Circlesong

Bob Chilcott

for upper voices, SATB, and piano
or 2 pianos and percussion

vocal score

MUSIC DEPARTMENT

OXFORD
UNIVERSITY PRESS

OXFORD
UNIVERSITY PRESS

Great Clarendon Street, Oxford OX2 6DP,
United Kingdom

Oxford University Press is a department of the University of Oxford.
It furthers the University's objective of excellence in research, scholarship,
and education by publishing worldwide. Oxford is a registered trade mark of
Oxford University Press in the UK and in certain other countries

First published 2020

ISBN 978-0-19-354043-9

Music and text origination by Katie Johnston

Printed in Great Britain on acid-free paper by
Halstan & Co. Ltd, Amersham, Bucks.

Contents

Scoring

This revised version of *Circlesong* is scored for upper voices and SATB.

A separate part for upper voices is also available (ISBN 978–0–19–354372–0).

Instrumentation

The accompaniment to this work exists in two versions:

For small ensemble

2 pianos and percussion (4 players):

      1. marimba

      2. tubular bells, triangle, wood blocks

      3. tam-tam, bongos

      4. timpani, hi-hat, tom-toms

Full scores, vocal scores, and instrumental parts are available on hire/rental from the publisher's Hire Library or appropriate agent. For small ensemble performances, the piano parts available on hire/rental should be used, rather than the part in the vocal score.

For one piano

The pianist plays from the vocal score.

Composer's note

I have found in my work, in my past as a singer and latterly as a composer, that an overwhelming sense of discovery, curiosity, inspiration, knowledge, and the desire to understand the rich tapestry of the human condition, has opened up to me through words that I have either sung or set. As someone who grew up singing the Christian liturgy on a daily basis, I have found great solace in setting Biblical texts, hymns, and psalms. I have also read and set a great deal of secular poetry in English and for a number of years have worked in collaboration with living poets. The text and the words become the vehicle for whatever musical discourse and picture I wish to present.

In the late 1990s I became very interested in indigenous poetry after reading a book of prayers (in English translation) from many different cultures. I set a number of these prayers and poems and, soon after, was inspired to write a larger work, a life-cycle piece based on translated poetry of indigenous tribes of North America; the text to *Circlesong* is drawn from the Chinook, Comanche, Dakota, Inuit, Iroquois, Kwakwaka'wakw, Navajo, Ojibwa, Pueblo, Seminole, Sioux, and Yaqui traditions. A recurring image in the poetry was that of a circle and I became fascinated by this. On a musical level the circle is the shape of the musical notehead, a written symbol that comes to life through sound. The circle is the shape of our world, of the sun, and of the moon. The circle symbolizes day and night, the pattern of the seasons, and the cyclical roundness of our natural world. The circle also symbolizes our interdependence and, most importantly, our unity as a human family. I found a beautiful poem, 'Song for Bringing a Child into the World,' written on the page in the shape of a circle and this set me on my way. I decided to cast this piece within a concept loosely modelled on the seven ages of man—Birth, Childhood, Lover, Adulthood, Middle Age, Old Age, Death—using these beautiful poems ultimately to articulate the importance of living life with care and respect, not only for our world but also for ourselves and each other, with all that that entails.

Circlesong was written in 2003 for the Birmingham Festival Choral Society and City of Birmingham Young Voices, and premiered in Birmingham, UK, in 2004. The work was revised in 2019 for Robert Simpson and the Houston Chamber Choir and the Treble Choir of Houston, and this version was first performed in Houston in February 2020. It is scored for upper-voice choir, mixed choir, two pianos, and four percussion players.

Duration: *c*.40 minutes

This note may be reproduced as required for programme notes.

Circlesong *was jointly funded by Arts Council West Midlands and the Birmingham Local Education Authority. It was first performed by BFCS and CBYV on 3 April 2004 in the Adrian Boult Hall, Birmingham, conducted by David Lawrence and Jeremy Patterson.*

Texts

1. Beauty before me/We wait in the darkness

Navajo/Iroquois

Beauty before me,
Beauty behind me.
Beauty, beauty.

We wait in the darkness!
Now no star is glowing;
Now no sun is shining;
Help in our journey.

Beauty below me,
Beauty above me.
Beauty, beauty.

2. Song for Bringing a Child into the World

Seminole

> Let the child be born
> circling around   you day sun
> you wrinkled skin   circling around
> circling around   you daylight
> you flecked with gray   circling around
> circling around   you night sun
> you wrinkled age   circling around
> circling around   you poor body

3. Newborn

Pueblo

Newborn, on the naked sand
Nakedly lay it
Next to the earth mother,
That it may know her;
Having good thoughts of her, the food giver.

Newborn, we tenderly
In our arms take it,
Making good thoughts.

Housegod, be entreated,
That it may grow from childhood to adulthood,
Happy, contented;
Beautifully walking
The trail to old age.

Having good thoughts of the earth its mother,
That she may give it the fruits of her being.
Newborn, on the naked sand
Nakedly lay it.

4. Yaqui Song

Yaqui

Many pretty flowers, red, blue, and yellow.
We say to the folk, 'Let us go and walk among the flowers.'
The wind comes and sways the flowers.
They all are like that when they dance.

Some are wide open, large flowers, and some are tiny little flowers.
The birds love the sunshine and the starlight.
The flowers smell sweet.
They all are sweeter than the flowers.

5. A Child's Song

Kwakwaka'wakw

When I am grown up
I shall go and stoop digging clams.
When I am grown up
I shall go and splash in the water digging clams.
When I am grown up
I shall stoop down digging clams.
When I am grown up
I shall go picking berries.

6. Give me strength

Sioux

Give me the strength to walk the soft earth.
Give me the eyes to see and the strength to understand
that I might be like you.
With your power only can I face the winds,
All over the earth we are all alike.

Look upon these faces of children without number
and with children in their arms.
With your power only can I face the winds
and walk the good road to the day of quiet.
Give me strength.

7. Chinook Songs

Chinook

Aya!

I don't care if you desert me,
Many other folk are in the town.
Soon I'll take another one,
That is not hard for me!

Whose sweetheart has gone away?
My sweetheart has gone away!
You do not like me!
I know you.

Very unhappy I was in Victoria.
Nobody said good-day to us in Victoria.

8. Over the Wave

Ojibwa

Who, my friend, makes this river flow?
The Spirit—he makes its ripples glow.
But I've a charm that can make the tide
Bring you over the wave to your lover's side.

Who, my friend, makes this river flow?
The Spirit—he makes its ripples glow.
Yet every blush that my love would hide,
Is mirror'd for me in the tell-tale tide.

And though you sleep on the farthest isle,
Round which these dimpling waters smile.
Yet I've a charm that can make the tide
Bring you over the wave to your lover's side.

9. Summer Song

Inuit

Aya! Aya! Ayaya.
It is beautiful when the summer comes at last.
Aya! Aya! Ayaya.
It is beautiful when the reindeer begin to come.
Aya! Aya! Ayaya.
When the roaring river rushes from the hills in summer.
Aya! Aya! Ayaya.

10. O Great Spirit

Dakota

O Great Spirit, whose voice speaks in the wind,
whose breath gives life to all the world.
Hear me!

I am small and weak, I need your power and wisdom,
Let me walk in beauty, let my eyes be glad
beholding the red and golden dawn.

Make my hands touch all things you have made with love,
Make me wise that I may understand the sacred teachings you have taught.
Help me, help me learn the lessons hidden in every leaf and every stone.

Help me, help me
I seek strength not to be greater than my brother
but to conquer the enemy within myself.

Make me ready to come to you always with a pure heart and with clear eyes,
so when my life fades away, like the setting sun,
my spirit may come to you with honour and without shame.

O Great Spirit, whose voice speaks in the wind,
whose breath gives life to all the world,
Hear me! Hear me! Hear me!

11. In the house made of dawn

Navajo

In the house made of dawn,
In the story made of dawn,
On the trail of dawn,
O talking God!

Your feet, my feet restore,
Your limbs, my limbs restore,
Your body, my body restore,
Your mind, my mind restore,
Your voice, my voice restore,
Your plumes, my plumes restore.

With beauty before you,
With beauty before me,
With beauty behind you,
With beauty behind me,
With beauty above you,
With beauty above me,
With beauty below you,
With beauty below me,
With beauty around you,
With beauty around me.

In the house of evening light,
From the story made of evening light,
On the trail of evening light,
It is finished in beauty.

12. Farewell, my brother

Navajo

Farewell, my brother,
When the showers pass over you,
And the thunder sounds.
And when the harvests ripen, and you hear voices
Of all the beautiful birds,
You will say, 'There is the trail of his soul.'

13. The sun's beams are running out/We wait in the darkness

Comanche/Iroquois

The sun's beams are running out.
The sun's yellow beams are running out.
The sun's beams are running out.

We wait in the darkness!
Now no star is glowing;
Now no sun is shining;
Come show us the pathway;
Help in our journey.

We shall live again,
We shall live again,
live again, again.

Circlesong

CIRCLESONG

BOB CHILCOTT

INTRODUCTION

1. Beauty before me / We wait in the darkness

Navajo / Iroquois

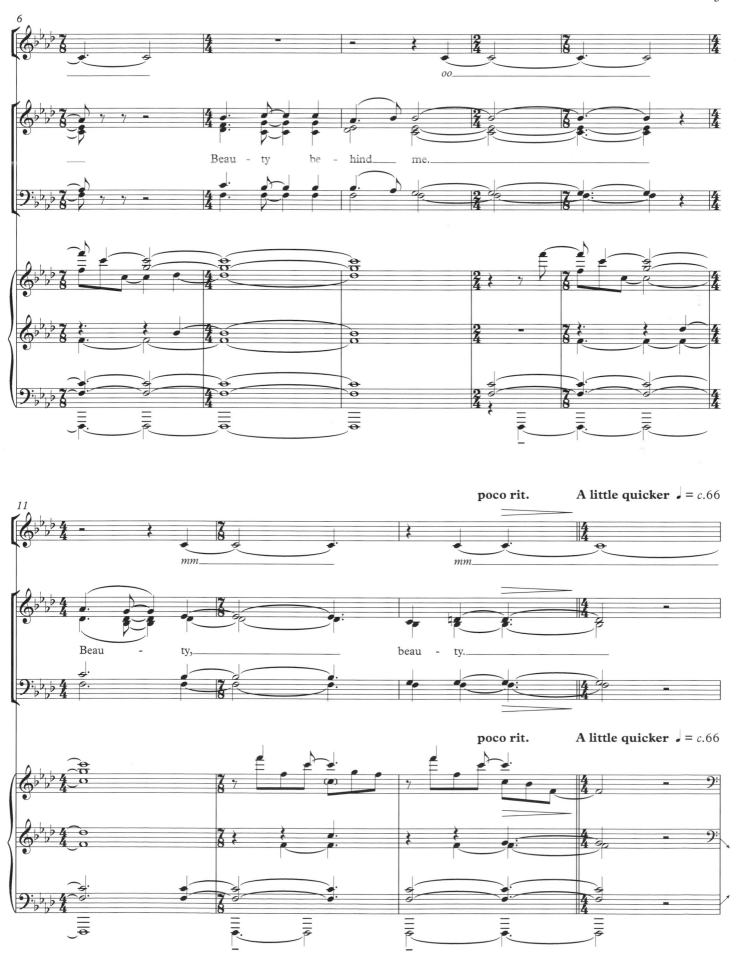

4

6

Show us the way; Our jour-

path-way; Help in our jour-ney.

-ney. No star,

Now no star is glow-ing; Now no sun is

PART 1: BIRTH

2. Song for Bringing a Child into the World

Seminole

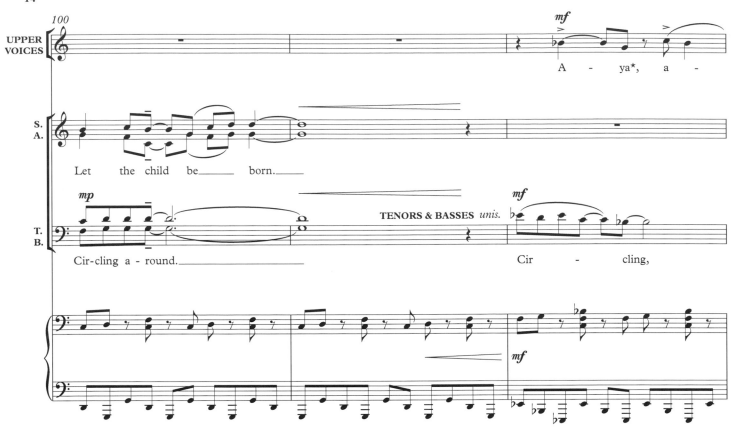

* pronounced 'eye-ya'

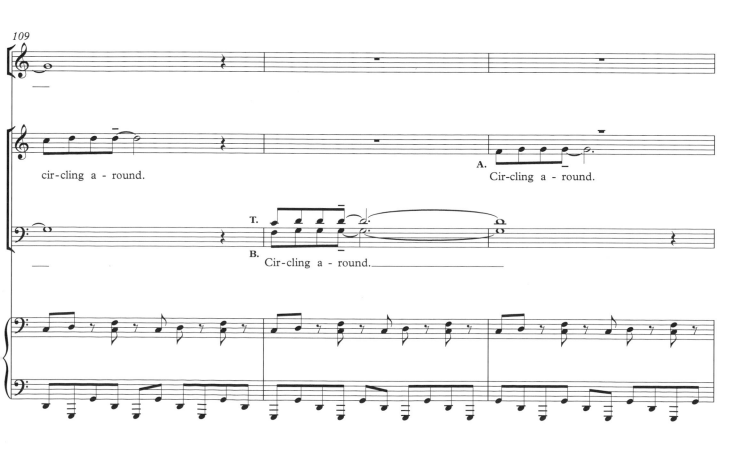

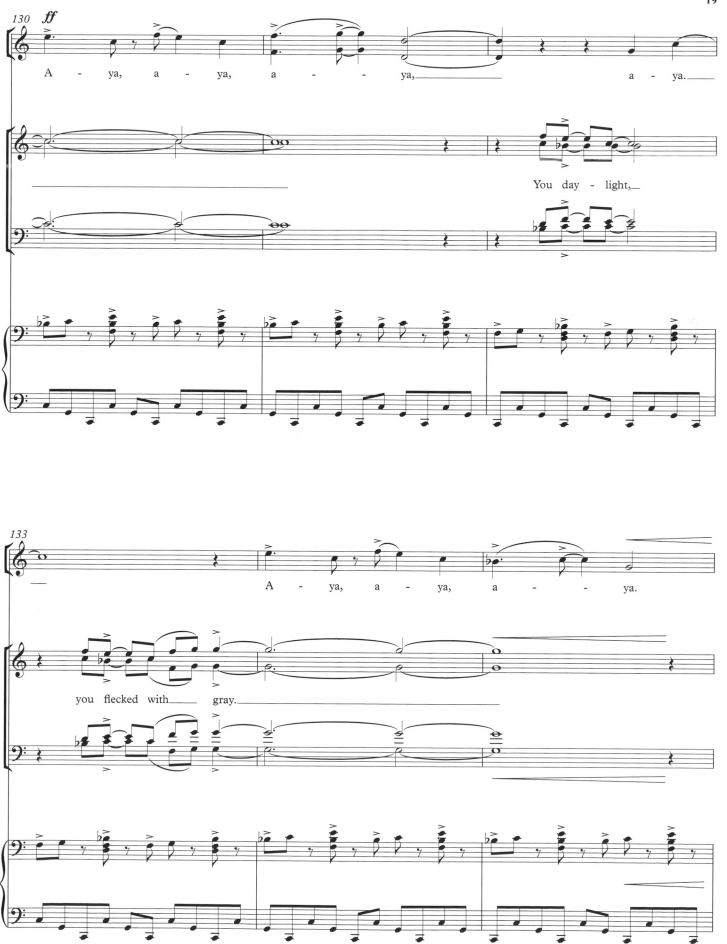

23

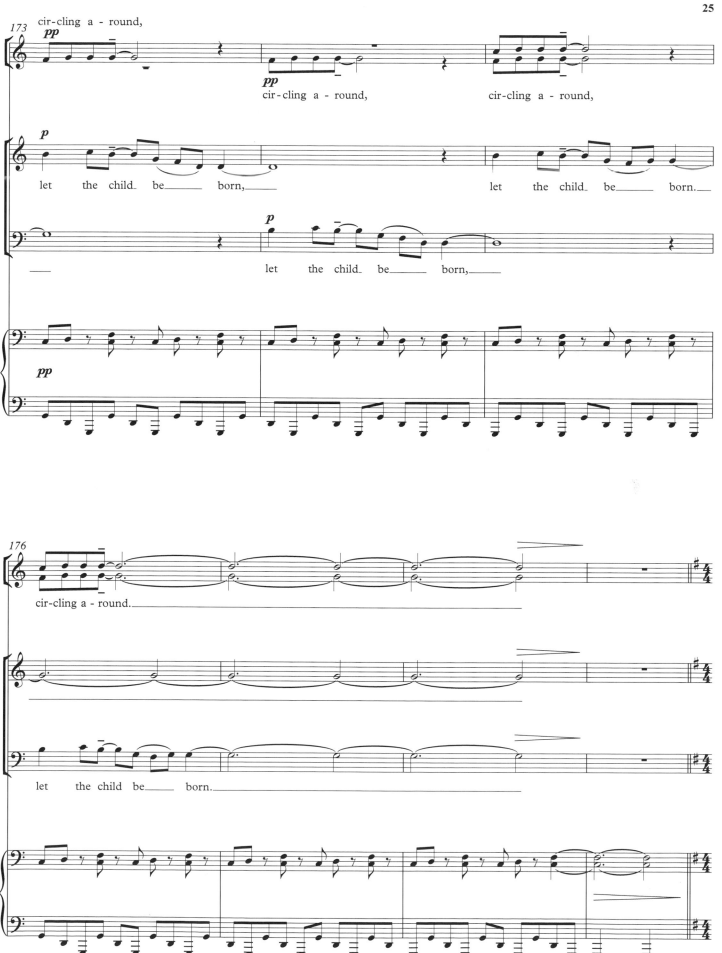

3. Newborn

Pueblo

Newborn, on the naked sand Nakedly lay it

Next to the earth mother,
Next to the earth, the earth mother, That it may know her;

Having good thoughts of her, the food giver. Newborn, we

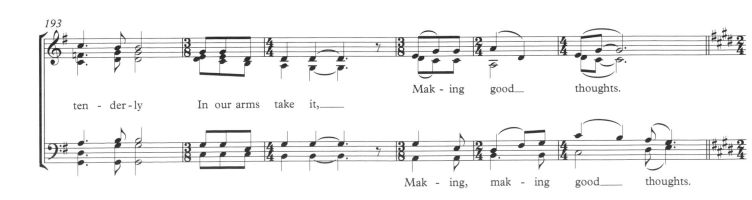

tenderly In our arms take it, Making good thoughts.
Making, making good thoughts.

PART 2: CHILDHOOD

4. Yaqui Song

Yaqui

Bright ♩ = *c*.92

UPPER VOICES

Ma - ny pret - ty flowers,___ red, blue and yel - low. We

PIANO

say to the folk, 'Let us go___ and walk a - mong the flowers.'___

The wind___ comes and sways the flowers.___

They all are like that when they dance.____

Some are wide o-pen, large flowers, and some are ti-ny lit-tle flowers. The

birds love the sun-shine and the star-light. The flowers smell sweet. The

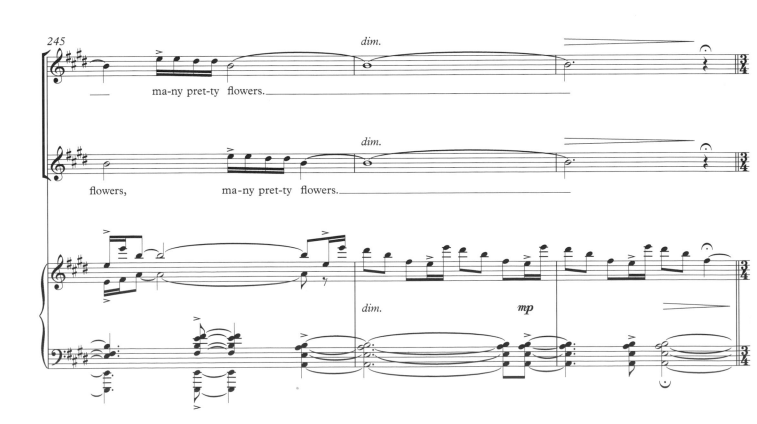

5. A Child's Song

Kwakwaka'wakw

attacca

6. Give me strength

Sioux

With a steady beat ♩ = c.72

UPPER
VOICES

SOPRANO
ALTO

oo

TENOR
BASS

Give me the   strength   to walk the

PIANO

With a steady beat ♩ = c.72

273

S.
A.

oo

T.
B.

soft   earth.   Give   me   the eyes   to   see   and the

276

oo

strength   to un - der - stand   that I   might   be   like   you.

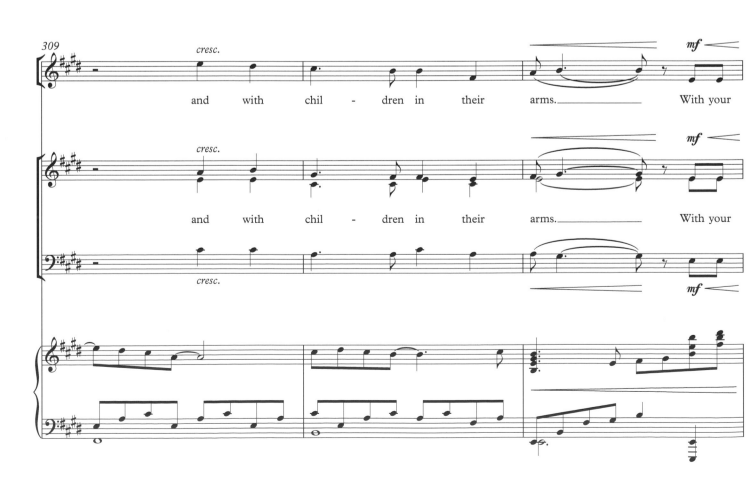

38

PART 3: LOVER

7. Chinook Songs

Chinook

* pronounced 'eye-ya'

40

8. Over the Wave

Ojibwa

Who, my friend, makes this ri-ver flow? The Spi-rit — he makes its rip-ples glow. But

I've a charm that can make the tide Bring you o-ver the wave to your lo-ver's side.

46

PART 4: ADULTHOOD

9. Summer Song

Inuit

* pronounced 'eye-ya'

When the roar-ing ri - ver rush-es from the hills in sum - mer.

-ya! A - ya! A -

When the ri - ver rush - es down.

A - ya! A - ya! A - ya! A - ya! A - ya! A - ya! A - ya! A - ya!

-ya!

A - ya! A - ya! A - ya! A - ya! A - ya

PART 5: MIDDLE AGE

10. O Great Spirit

Dakota

60

558

eyes be glad be-hold - ing the red and gold-en dawn.

eyes be glad be-hold - ing the red and gold-en dawn, red and gold-en dawn.

be-hold - ing the red and gold-en, red and gold-en dawn, gold-en dawn.

be-hold - ing the red and gold-en dawn, the red and

562

Gold - en dawn.

Make my hands touch

gold-en dawn. Make my hands touch

PART 6: OLD AGE

11. In the house made of dawn

Navajo

* pronounced 'eye-ya'

† The piano reduction excludes the upper voices' parts for reasons of playability.

638

74

675

78

695

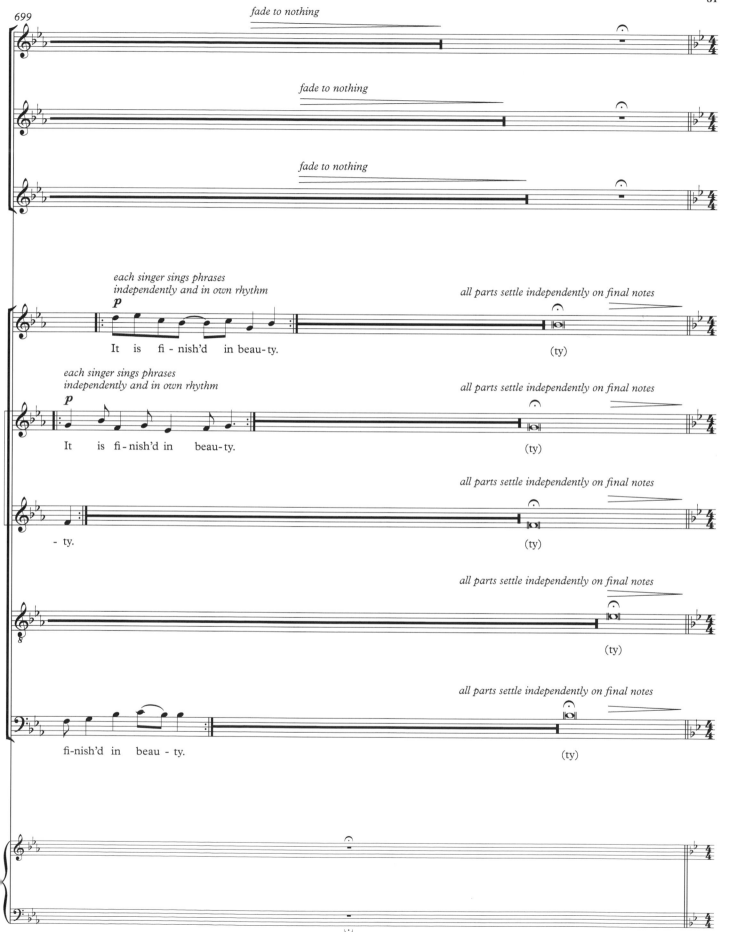

82

PART 7: DEATH

12. Farewell, my brother

Navajo

84

13. *The sun's beams are running out / We wait in the darkness*

Comanche / Iroquois

* Small notes are for rehearsal only.

93